# SCARY PLACES
# Abandoned
# Insane Asylums

by Dinah Williams

Consultant: Troy Taylor
President of the American Ghost Society

BEARPORT
PUBLISHING

New York, New York

## Credits

Cover and Title Page, © Jeremiah Deasey/istockphoto.com, Jonathan Torgovnik/CORBIS, © Robert Sciarrino/Star Ledger/Corbis, and © Jerry Cooke/CORBIS; 4–5, © Robert Sciarrino/Star Ledger/Corbis; 6, © Mary Evans Picture Library/Alamy; 7, © Private Collection, The Stapleton Collection/The Bridgeman Art Library; 8, © Bettmann/CORBIS; 9, © Missouri Valley Special Collections, Kansas City Public Library, Kansas City, Missouri; 10, © Foxie Hagerty; 11A, © Foxie Hagerty; 11B, © Phil Schermeister/CORBIS; 12, Provided courtesy of Ethan McElroy; 13, Courtesy of Andy Henderson; 14A, © Steve Bronstein/The Image Bank/Getty Images; 14B, © Bettmann/CORBIS; 15, Courtesy of Wikimedia Foundation, Inc.; 16, © Eric Tomenga; 17, © Jerry Cooke/Time & Life Pictures/Getty Images; 18A, © Matt Plante-Fallout-UE.com; 18B, © Matt Plante-Fallout-UE.com; 19A, © SR/Shutterstock; 19B, © James Stevenson/Photo Researchers, Inc.; 19C, © Ljupco Smokovski/Shutterstock; 20, © Alexander Turnbull Library; 21, © Bettmann/CORBIS; 22, © Saul Beeson/Saul Beeson Photography; 23A, © Saul Beeson/Saul Beeson Photography; 23B, © Saul Beeson/Saul Beeson Photography; 24A, © Provided courtesy of Ethan McElroy; 24B, © Provided courtesy of Ethan McElroy; 25A, © The Granger Collection, New York; 25B, © The Granger Collection, New York; 26A, © North Wind Picture Archives; 26B, © Jerry Cooke/Photo Researchers, Inc.; 27, © Courtesy of historicasylums.com; 31, © Lagui/Shutterstock.

Publisher: Kenn Goin
Editorial Director: Adam Siegel
Creative Director: Spencer Brinker
Design: Dawn Beard Creative
Photo Researcher: Beaura Kathy Ringrose

*Library of Congress Cataloging-in-Publication Data*

Williams, Dinah.
 Abandoned insane asylums : by Dinah Williams.
    p. cm. — (Scary places)
 Includes bibliographical references and index.
 ISBN-13: 978-1-59716-575-4 (library binding)
 ISBN-10: 1-59716-575-1 (library binding)
 1. Asylums—History—Juvenile literature. 2. Psychiatric hospitals—History—Juvenile literature. 3. Mental health care—History—Juvenile literature. I. Title.

 RC439.W537 2008
 362.2'1—dc22

                    2007038531

For more information, write to Bearport Publishing Company, Inc., 101 Fifth Avenue, Suite 6R, New York, New York, 10003. Printed in the United States of America.

10 9 8 7 6 5 4 3 2 1

# Contents

# Abandoned Insane Asylums

Some people have a hard time knowing the difference between what is real and what is imaginary. These **mentally ill** people may hear voices or see things that aren't really there. They may also mistakenly think people are trying to hurt them.

In the past, doctors didn't understand the causes and cures for mental illness. As a result, many of their treatments could be painful. Few were successful. Doctors often placed their patients in **asylums** that were overcrowded and dirty. These places could be more like prisons than hospitals.

Today, the causes of mental illness are better understood. The treatments are better, too. Many of the asylums of the past have been **abandoned**. The memories of the patients' pain, however, still linger within their walls. In the 11 abandoned asylums in this book, you'll discover some of the most terrifying and terrible hospitals for the mentally ill. Luckily, they have all been closed.

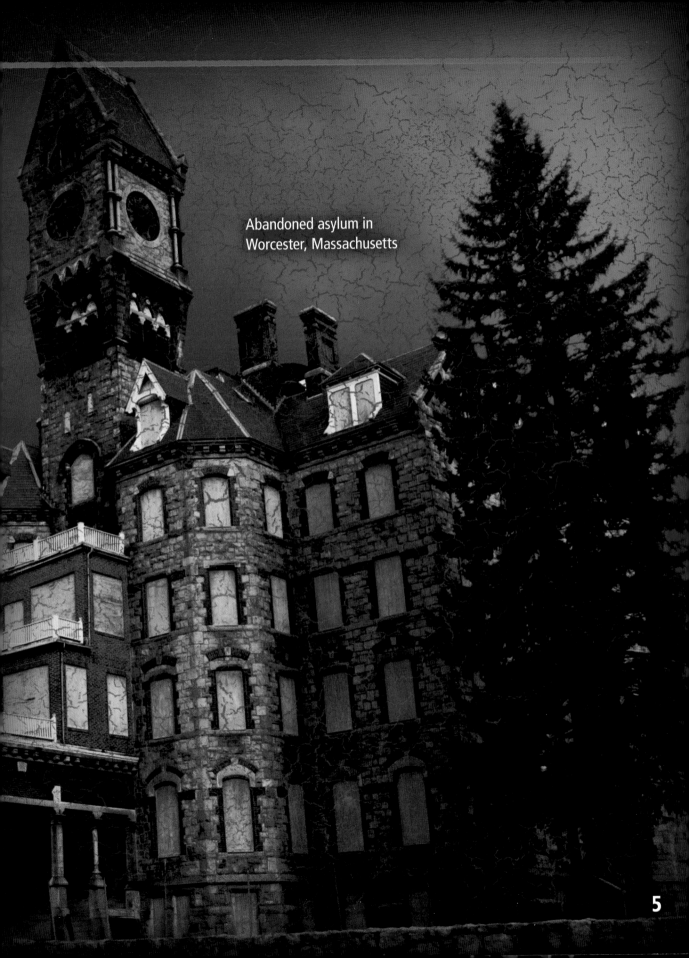

Abandoned asylum in
Worcester, Massachusetts

# Bedlam at Bethlem

## Bethlem Royal Hospital, Moorfields, London, England
### Opened 1676 • Closed 1815

In the 1700s, many people thought that mental illness was caused by evil **spirits**. Some doctors thought it could never be cured. As a result, patients at asylums were often locked away in cages and treated like animals. For a large part of its history, Bethlem Royal Hospital was such a place. Here, the mentally ill were kept—not treated.

Patients and visitors at Bethlem Royal Hospital in the 1700s

The Bethlem Royal Hospital in Bishopsgate, London, began caring for the mentally ill in 1403. The "care" mainly involved chaining patients to the floor or a wall. They were beaten when they couldn't be controlled. By the middle of the 1600s, the hospital was overcrowded and dirty. So in 1676 the patients were moved to a larger building in a different part of London, called Moorfields.

At Moorfields, the mentally ill became a tourist attraction. People paid a penny to laugh at the "**lunatics**." Visitors were allowed to bring long sticks to poke **inmates** chained in their cells. In 1814, about 96,000 people visited the asylum. The next year, the building had become so run-down that the patients were moved to a new hospital in St. George's Fields. While this new asylum looked better, the treatment of the patients was nearly as bad.

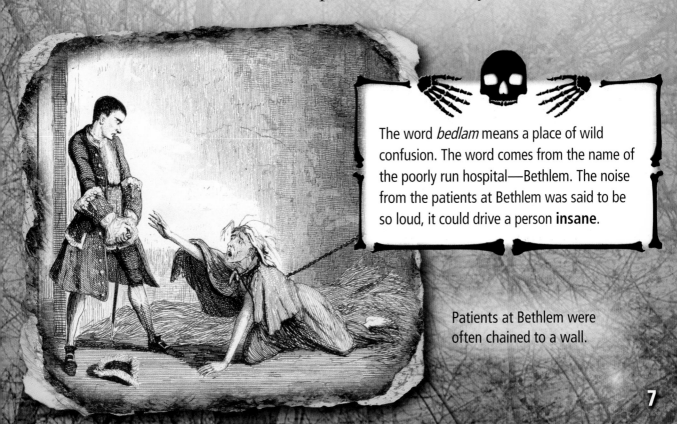

The word *bedlam* means a place of wild confusion. The word comes from the name of the poorly run hospital—Bethlem. The noise from the patients at Bethlem was said to be so loud, it could drive a person **insane**.

Patients at Bethlem were often chained to a wall.

7

# A Doctor Is "Cured"

## Christian Church Hospital, Kansas City, Missouri
### Opened 1914 • Closed 1975

Doctors in the mid-1900s would sometimes perform **lobotomies** to calm violent patients. In this surgery, a sharp instrument is forced into the brain through the **eye socket**. The doctor then cuts **nerve** connections in the brain. Studies later showed that the operation harmed many more people than it helped.

A doctor performing a lobotomy in the 1940s

Between 1939 and 1951, as many as 18,000 people in the United States had lobotomies.

In 1927, Dr. Robert Patterson bought the Christian Church Hospital. He was known to be a skilled doctor but not a kind man. For 30 years, he used terrible treatments to try to "cure" his mentally ill patients. Some were beaten. Others were chained to their beds. If the patients could not be controlled, he performed **ice pick** lobotomies on them. Many ended up with brain damage.

In 1957, Dr. Patterson suddenly went insane. All attempts to help him failed. Finally, Patterson's staff used his favorite cure—an ice pick lobotomy. He died soon afterward. The hospital was then sold so it could be turned into apartments. Perhaps people will finally be able to live peacefully in the building.

Christian Church Hospital

# The Tree of Tears

## Bartonville Insane Asylum, Bartonville, Illinois
### Opened 1902 • Closed 1972

Many of the patients at Bartonville Insane Asylum spent most of their lives there. It was the only home they knew. Some who died at the hospital were buried there, too. They were often **mourned** by the man who some say "lives" there still.

Bartonville Insane Asylum

In the early 1900s, a man called Bookbinder was a patient at the Bartonville Insane Asylum. Dr. George Zeller, who ran the hospital, had him work as a gravedigger at the hospital's **cemetery**.

Every time Bookbinder helped bury a patient, he would cry. Often he would lean against an old elm tree as he sobbed.

When Bookbinder died in 1910, most of the staff attended his **funeral**. As they put his **coffin** in the ground, the staff heard a wail coming from the old elm. People turned to find out who had made the noise. Next to the tree they saw a shocking sight. There was Bookbinder, crying his eyes out.

Was the dead man no longer in his coffin? Dr. Zeller quickly opened it to see. Bookbinder's body was still inside. When people looked back at the elm, his ghost had disappeared.

Graves at Bartonville

The old elm at Bartonville Insane Asylum began to die soon after Bookbinder's funeral. When workmen started chopping down the dying tree, they heard a cry of pain. So they tried burning the tree instead. The sound of sobbing, however, caused them to quickly put out the flames.

# Lost But Not Forgotten

## Athens Mental Health Center, Athens, Ohio
### Opened 1874 • Closed 1993

Around three million soldiers fought in the U.S. **Civil War** (1861–1865).
After the war ended, many of the men suffered from nightmares
and painful memories. At times their problems were overwhelming.
Several huge asylums were built to help treat them and other
patients. Some of the buildings were so big that a person could
easily become lost in them.

Athens Mental Health Center

KENNEDY MUSEUM OF ART

On December 1, 1978, one of the patients at Athens Mental Health Center disappeared. Her name was Margaret Schilling. A search party was formed to find her. They looked in each of the huge building's 544 rooms. Yet no trace of Margaret was found.

Weeks later, a janitor made a shocking discovery. Margaret was found dead in the attic, where she must have been hiding. Unable to care for herself, Margaret probably died from **starvation**, or from the cold temperatures in the unheated room.

Margaret's body was removed, but a detailed outline of it remained on the marble floor. The folds of her clothes and the style of her hair could easily be seen. The floor was cleaned over and over again, but the stain wouldn't go away. It can still be seen there today.

Due to overcrowding at Athens in the early 1900s, many patients were often forced to sleep together in rooms that were meant for one person. As they lay there, hour after hour, some would carve messages on their windowsills. One that can still be seen reads "I was never crazy."

The outline of Margaret's body

# The Scary Sounds of Soft Walls

## Fremantle Lunatic Asylum, Fremantle, Australia
### Opened 1860s • Closed early 1900s

Violent patients at asylums were often placed in special cells. These rooms had no furniture. The walls and floors were covered with soft padding to stop patients from harming themselves on hard or sharp edges. The Fremantle Lunatic Asylum had one such padded cell for its most difficult inmates. Although the asylum was closed about 100 years ago, some say that the cell may not be empty.

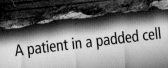

A patient in a padded cell

Padded cells were also called "rubber rooms."

Visitors to the Fremantle History Museum can easily see signs of the gloomy building's original use. Past a thick wooden door lies the former asylum's padded cell. Bars line the room's window. Visitors can still see the **peephole** on the door that doctors used to spy on their patients.

Built by prisoners in the 1860s, the former lunatic asylum is considered one of Australia's most haunted places. The gloomy padded cell, where the most violent patients were kept, has frightened more than one visitor. A local historian who toured it heard the voice of a young woman screaming "No! No! No!" When her friend touched the door, the voice screamed, "Don't shut it!" She left the door open.

Fremantle Lunatic Asylum

# A Small City of Misery

**Philadelphia State Hospital at Byberry, Philadelphia, Pennsylvania**

Opened early 1900s • Closed 1990

Like many asylums, Byberry began with the noble goal of helping the mentally ill. Set on 200 acres (81 hectares) of land, it was a working farm where patients grew their own food. Overcrowding and lack of money, however, soon turned the asylum into a place of **misery**.

Philadelphia State Hospital at Byberry

Albert Deutsch wrote a book about insane asylums in 1948. In it, he described Byberry as "a building swarming with naked humans herded like cattle." He wrote that the asylum's smell was so terrible and strong one could almost see it. At that time, Byberry had at least 6,000 patients.

Even with more than 50 buildings, Byberry was one of the most overcrowded and **neglected** asylums in America. The hospital was given so little money for clothes by the city of Philadelphia that some patients wore nothing at all. With little staff, patients were left tied to their beds. Stories of **abuse** continued until the governor ordered the asylum shut down in 1987. It finally closed its doors in 1990.

William Kirsch was a patient at Byberry. In 1987, people inspecting the asylum learned that he had been tied to a bed for 14 months.

A crowded asylum in the 1940s

# Murder at the Metropolitan

## Metropolitan State Hospital, Waltham, Massachusetts
### Opened 1930 • Closed 1992

Large asylums cared for many types of mentally ill patients. Some people heard voices when no one was talking. Others believed they saw things that weren't really there. A small number were even capable of murder. Such was the case with Melvin Wilson.

Metropolitan State Hospital

18

On August 9, 1978, Anne Marie Davee was granted a pass to walk around Metropolitan State Hospital, where she was a patient. When she didn't return, the grounds were searched. Doctors assumed she had wandered off. Months passed with no sign of her. Hospital workers did, however, find her purse. It contained sunglasses and photographs. There was also a small ax inside!

The police soon realized how the ax was connected to Anne Marie. A fellow patient, Melvin Wilson, had used it to kill her. He had chopped up her body and buried it in three shallow **graves** near the hospital. He had also kept seven of Anne Marie's teeth. On August 12, 1980, Wilson led investigators to her body. He was later charged with murder—and sent to another mental hospital.

In the early 1960s, children suffering from mental illness were treated at Metropolitan. It is rumored that the doctors accidentally poisoned more than two dozen of them. They had put a chemical in the children's milk, believing it would treat their illness. It killed them instead.

# Trapped by Fire

## Seacliff Lunatic Asylum, Seacliff, New Zealand
### Opened 1884 • Closed 1973

During World War II (1939–1945), many nurses left their jobs at mental hospitals to care for wounded soldiers. This left some asylums with a much smaller staff than they needed. So what happens when there is an emergency at a mental hospital and there aren't enough workers? In 1942, the patients of Seacliff Lunatic Asylum found out.

Seacliff Lunatic Asylum

On December 9, 1942, the female patients in Ward 5 of the Seacliff Lunatic Asylum were locked in their rooms for the night. There was a shortage of nurses at the hospital, so none were on duty that evening. At 9:45 P.M., a male worker finally noticed that the wooden building was in flames. The hospital firefighters battled the fierce blaze. However, they were only able to save two patients. After an hour, Ward 5 was a pile of smoking ashes. Thirty-seven women were dead.

The fire, one of the worst in New Zealand's history, damaged only one building at Seacliff. So the asylum was able to continue caring for its patients. The treatment there, however, was as cruel as at other asylums of the time. Patients were beaten and given lobotomies. Many tried to run away. The asylum, however, kept taking in new ones.

Electroshock therapy was widely used at Seacliff. In this treatment, developed in the 1930s, an electric current is sent through a patient's brain. Although electroshock therapy was misused in the past, doctors today think that it can in fact help some mentally ill people.

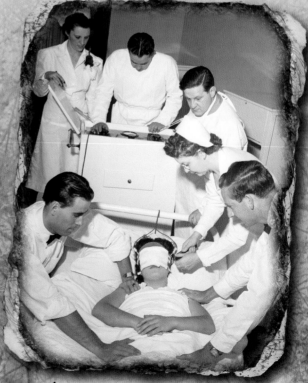

A patient receiving electroshock therapy in the 1940s

21

# Taking the Care Out of Caring

## Whittingham Hospital, Whittingham, England
### Opened 1893 • Closed 1995

Like many asylums in the 1800s, Whittingham was created to care for the mentally ill. Unlike other asylums, it had its own train station, brass band, orchestra, post office, and church. How did a place so thoughtfully designed turn into a place so unfeeling?

Whittingham Hospital

In 1967, a collection of articles and essays called *Sans Everything* (*Without Everything*) was published. The book described the cruel ways mentally ill patients were treated at asylums. The author could easily have been describing life at Whittingham. The rooms in this asylum were damp and cold. They were also crawling with cockroaches and ants. Some patients were locked in small rooms or bathrooms. Others were left outside, regardless of the weather.

The staff would sometimes beat patients and tie them to chairs. Workers calmed down patients using the "wet towel treatment." This involved twisting a wet towel around a patient's neck until he or she passed out. Nurses were even accused of setting fire to a patient's clothes while they were being worn!

Whittingham had a lot of activities for patients, and it looked lovely. Without a caring staff, however, it was just a pretty prison.

The inside of Whittingham after it was abandoned

During World War II, Whittingham had more than 3,000 patients. This made it the largest asylum in England at that time.

# The Cold Bath Cure

**Dixmont State Hospital, Kilbuck Township, Pennsylvania**
### Opened 1862 • Closed 1984

Dorothea Dix was horrified by the treatment of the mentally ill in the 1800s. She traveled around the United States trying to educate people on how to properly care for them. She also helped found Dixmont State Hospital. While it was one of the better mental hospitals, painful treatments were still used there.

Dixmont State Hospital

Between 1840 and 1890, the number of mentally ill patients in U.S. hospitals grew from about 2,561 to 74,000. Many of these were **veterans** of the U.S. Civil War. They suffered from upsetting memories about the bloody battles in which they had fought. These men crowded the country's asylums, including Dixmont. By 1900, the hospital had more than 1,200 patients. Unfortunately, the staff didn't always know how to cure them.

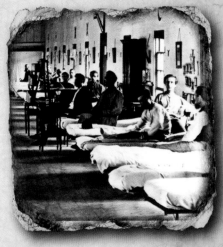
Wounded Civil War soldiers

One terrible treatment doctors tried was called hydrotherapy. It consisted of being placed for hours in a freezing or hot bath. Sometimes ice packs would be placed on patients' heads to further shock their systems. **Bandages** might also be wrapped around their eyes and ears to block out any sound or light. Surprisingly, this treatment was supposed to calm patients down.

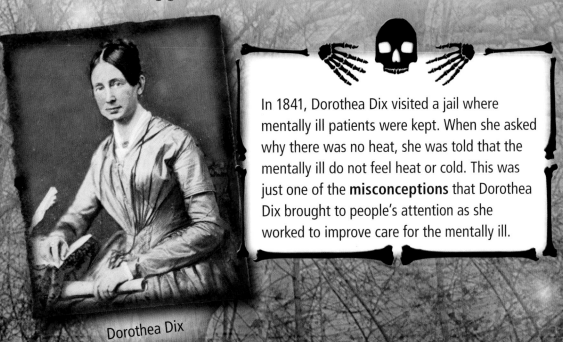

In 1841, Dorothea Dix visited a jail where mentally ill patients were kept. When she asked why there was no heat, she was told that the mentally ill do not feel heat or cold. This was just one of the **misconceptions** that Dorothea Dix brought to people's attention as she worked to improve care for the mentally ill.

Dorothea Dix

25

# Ghosts That Won't Be Tied Down

## Monson State Hospital, Palmer, Massachusetts
### Opened 1852 • Closed 1950s

A straitjacket has extra long sleeves that can be tied around the back. The sleeves keep a person's arms close to his or her chest and stop them from moving. In the 1800s, straitjackets were often used to keep patients from harming themselves or others. Unfortunately, many other methods were used to control patients as well.

A straightjacket

It is easy to imagine how awful it was to be locked away at Monson State Hospital. There is evidence everywhere of how former patients were tied down. Chains that held them are still bolted to the walls. Dusty chairs have arm cuffs that made sure patients sat still. Even the bathtubs have straps that were wrapped around patients' wrists and necks.

Most of the buildings on the sprawling Monson State Hospital grounds are long abandoned. So why are doors shutting and floors creaking? Maybe the noises are caused by the ghosts of the criminally insane who were once housed there.

Monson State Hospital

Today, more than 55 million adult Americans suffer from some type of mental illness. Many of these people can now be effectively treated with medication.

27

## Bartonville Insane Asylum
**Bartonville, Illinois**

The graveyard was haunted by the ghost of a patient who was also the gravedigger.

## Monson State Hospital
**Palmer, Massachusetts**

Patients were tied down, but ghosts roam free.

## Metropolitan State Hospital
**Waltham, Massachusetts**

A patient is not missing but murdered.

NORTH
AMERICA

## Christian Church Hospital
**Kansas City, Missouri**

Lobotomies were a common treatment.

## Philadelphia State Hospital at Byberry
**Philadelphia, Pennsylvania**

Patients were so neglected they didn't have clothes.

AFRICA

## Athens Mental Health Center
**Athens, Ohio**

The outline of a lost patient appears on the floor.

## Dixmont State Hospital
**Kilbuck Township, Pennsylvania**

Ice baths were used to calm patients.

Atlantic
Ocean

SOUTH
AMERICA

Pacific
Ocean

# Around the World

Arctic Ocean

EUROPE

ASIA

## Whittingham Hospital
**Whittingham, England**

Patients got the "wet towel treatment."

## Bethlem Royal Hospital
**London, England**

People paid to laugh at the inmates.

Indian Ocean

AUSTRALIA

## Fremantle Lunatic Asylum
**Fremantle, Australia**

Visitors can tour a haunted padded cell.

## Seacliff Lunatic Asylum
**Seacliff, New Zealand**

A fire killed patients locked in their rooms.

Southern Ocean

ANTARCTICA

# Glossary

**abandoned** (uh-BAN-duhnd) left empty; no longer used

**abuse** (uh-BYOOSS) harmful treatment

**asylums** (uh-SYE-luhmz) hospitals that take care of people who are mentally ill

**bandages** (BAN-dij-iz) pieces of cloth that are wrapped around injured parts of a body

**cemetery** (SEM-uh-*ter*-ee) an area of land where dead bodies are buried

**Civil War** (SIV-il WOR) the U.S. war between the Northern and Southern states that lasted from 1861 to 1865

**coffin** (KAWF-in) a container in which a dead person is placed for burying

**eye socket** (EYE SOK-it) a bony hole in the skull that surrounds and protects the eyeball

**funeral** (FYOO-nuh-ruhl) a ceremony that is held after a person dies

**graves** (GRAYVZ) holes dug in the ground where dead people are buried

**ice pick** (EYESS PIK) a sharp tool used for chipping away at chunks of ice

**inmates** (IN-mayts) people who are forced to live in an asylum, a prison, or some other kind of building

**insane** (in-SAYN) mentally ill

**lobotomies** (loh-BOT-uh-meez) surgical procedures meant to calm violent people; a sharp instrument is forced into the brain through the eye socket in order to cut some of the nerve connections in the patient's brain

**lunatics** (LOON-uh-tiks) a term that is used to describe mentally ill people in a negative way

**mentally ill** (MEN-tuhl-ee IL) having a mind that is not working normally

**misconceptions** (*mis*-kon-SEP-shunz) mistaken thoughts or ideas

**misery** (MIH-zuh-ree) great unhappiness

**mourned** (MORND) felt very sad over someone who died

**neglected** (ni-GLEKT-id) failed to take care of something or someone

**nerve** (NURV) one of the many fibers that sends messages between a person's brain and other parts of his or her body

**peephole** (PEEP-hohl) a small hole through which a person secretly looks at something

**spirits** (SPIHR-its) supernatural creatures, such as ghosts

**starvation** (star-VAY-shun) the act of dying from lack of food

**veterans** (VET-ur-uhnz) people who have served in the armed forces

# Bibliography

**Taylor, Troy, and Len Adams.** *So, There I Was . . .* Alton, IL: Whitechapel Productions Press (2006).

**Whitaker, Robert.** *Mad in America: Bad Science, Bad Medicine, and the Enduring Mistreatment of the Mentally Ill.* Cambridge, MA: Perseus Publishing (2002).

# Read More

**Banks, Cameron.** *America's Most Haunted.* New York: Scholastic (2002).

**Kent, Deborah.** *Snake Pits, Talking Cures & Magic Bullets: A History of Mental Illness.* Brookfield, CT: Twenty-First Century Books (2003).

**Witteman, Barbara.** *Dorothea Dix: Social Reformer.* Mankato, MN: Bridgestone Books (2003).

# Learn More Online

To learn more about abandoned asylums, visit
**www.bearportpublishing.com/ScaryPlaces**

# Index

# About the Author

Dinah Williams is a nonfiction editor and writer who has
produced dozens of books for children. She lives in New Jersey.